Design: Curtis McGlinchey and Linda McGlinchey.
Proofreading: James McGlinchey.
Editor: Curtis McGlinchey.

A catalogue record for this book is available from the
British Library.

ISBN: 978-0-9934529-3-2

Printed and bound in Wales, Great Britain
by Gomer Press.

This book was commissioned by Action Oak
and published by Garden World Images Ltd.

www.actionoak.org
www.igpoty.com

Cover photography © John Glover.

Photography on this page © Carolyne Barber.

Contents

Judges

Tyrone McGlinchey, Managing Director of the International Garden Photographer of the Year.

Tony Kirkham, Head of Arboretum and Horticultural Services, Royal Botanic Gardens, Kew.

Professor Nicola Spence, Chief Plant Health Officer, Department for Environment, Food & Rural Affairs.

Sir Harry Studholme, Chair of the Forestry Commission.

Celebrating Our Oaks_____

Action Oak is protecting our oaks for future generations, raising vital funds to research and manage our oak trees and woodlands. Launched at the RHS Chelsea Flower Show in May 2018, this new initiative is a unique collaboration of environmental bodies, charities, governments and landowners working together.

The oak tree holds a very special place in the hearts and minds of people, not only is it culturally and economically important, it contributes greatly to our sense of well-being; losing it would be devastating.

There are over 121 million oaks in the UK, and more ancient oaks than the rest of Europe combined. These include the globally important Atlantic oak woodland, our temperate rainforest, as well as ancient parkland trees. The benefits they bring are priceless for biodiversity; as a foundation species the oak supports over 2200 other species and is the UK's most important tree for biodiversity.

Our iconic oaks are under threat and we must act now to protect this iconic tree for the future; pests and diseases are challenging its very survival.

But if we can raise significant funds now, Action Oak can make a huge difference for the oak, helping:

• Scientists to better understand the threats oaks face and how they can best be overcome;
• People who own and manage oaks to apply that knowledge to give oaks a more secure future;
• All of us record how our local oaks are doing, so that what we see today can help shape how the oak does tomorrow.

This programme of vital research and monitoring into the threats oaks are facing will build upon the ground-breaking research being undertaken already, that has not only helped us to understand the oak much better than before, but which has also revealed just how much there still is to learn, if we are to protect these much-loved trees for future generations.

Action Oak would like to thank the National Trust for generously supporting Celebrating Our Oaks and finally thank you for purchasing this book. All profits raised go direct to Action Oak, which means they can continue working toward celebrating and saving our oak trees. Thank you.

Find more information at www.actionoak.org

Foreword

by Dame Judi Dench

I have always had an affinity with trees. As a child, I loved oaks for no particular reason other than it was a wonderful tree to climb. Imagine my delight when I was shown a stained glass window in a church in Sandymount, Dublin – dedicated to Bessie Oak Smith, my paternal grandmother! So it is no wonder that this of all trees is so close to my heart.

I first met Tony Kirkham when I started filming 'My Passion for Trees'. He came to my house and we measured the wonderful mature English oak in my garden that I treasure so much.

Through his knowledge, we measured the trunk and worked out its age and I discovered that it had been there since the time of the Battle of Waterloo (1812-ish). He estimated that if all the branches were laid end-to-end, they would measure 15 miles, and the leaves would have covered two tennis courts. I also learned that any oak has so much supporting it under the ground in root mass as there is above the ground, albeit very shallow and mine drinks at least two bathtubs full of water every day.

I love all trees and plant lots – on the birth of my grandson Sam, we planted an oak sapling in the garden. He is now 21 and 6ft tall, but his oak is now six times as tall as he is and still growing.

The oak is an amazing tree and has been used down the centuries for almost everything, from furniture to barrels to corks, not to mention the Mary Rose and Viking longships. A variety of birds love to nest in oaks and feed on the many insects that they support.

Shakespeare mentions oaks in his plays, in particular 'The Merry Wives of Windsor' when Falstaff is lured by Mistress Ford and Mistress Page to Hearn's oak.

I believe there are around 600 species of oak that grow around the world, but only two are native to England, which is very surprising. Acorns only grow once a tree is 40 years old, and they take 18 months to mature.

Now we have this beautiful book made up of a collection of winning photographs of oaks from an IGPOTY competition and celebrity favourites to celebrate the important work of Action Oak, a new initiative raising vital funds and awareness for further research and monitoring to help us save the mighty oak for future generations to cherish and enjoy.

I hope that you enjoy the book as much as I have.

ActionOak
PROTECTING OUR OAK TREES

Introduction

by Tony Kirkham,
Head of Arboretum and Horticultural Services,
Royal Botanic Gardens, Kew

The oak is the quintessential, iconic tree of the British landscape and rightly so, with over 121 million oaks growing in our woodlands, so it's no wonder that it's Britain's national tree. No other tree species would be able to fill the roots of the mighty oak. Of the 600-different species of oak that grow around the world, I have many favourites that I grow in the scientific collections in the arboretum at Kew, but seeing the oak growing in its natural habitat anywhere in the native woodlands of the northern hemisphere is one of the many humbling experiences that has encouraged me to work with trees. Whether it's the cork oak (*Quercus suber*) in the montado forests of Portugal or the red oak (*Quercus rubra*) in the rich temperate broadleaved forests of eastern North America especially in the fall, they all have a role to play in our daily lives.

We only have two species of oak that are native to our island, *Quercus robur*, the pedunculate oak, which is named for the strength of its hard timber, and *Quercus petraea*, the sessile oak. Both similar in general appearance, but each one with its own character. Historically, the timber and the products that they have provided us with over time have played a huge part in the making of Britain as the nation that it is today, whether it be through house building, furniture making, ship building, the clothes that we wear or Scotch whisky, to name but a few; It most probably has more uses for us than any other British native tree.

The oak is a long-lived species that can live for an average of 250 years, but there are many older specimens growing around the country, living to be over 400 years old which we call ancient oaks. In fact, there are over 3,300 listed ancient native oaks in England alone, which is more than all the ancient oaks growing in the rest of the European countries put together. These venerable trees have wide, stunted crowns, squat hollow trunks and are full of dead wood, providing an incredible resource and habitat for our native biodiversity with over 2,000 species of fungi, ferns, lichens, insects, birds and mammals living in them with more than 300 that are obligate species, only living on the English oak. That's more than any other tree species. Many of these ancient oaks are famous in their own right and are well-named. Probably one of the most famous and well known is the Major Oak in Sherwood Forest in which Robin Hood and his merry men hid from the Sherriff of Nottingham. Each and every one of them have their own tales to tell.

Unfortunately, our oaks are now under serious threat from exotic pests, such as the grey squirrel preventing our newly planted young oaks from establishing and reaching maturity and the oak processionary moth, *Thaumetopoea processionea*, a moth whose caterpillar can defoliate mature oaks. There are diseases such as acute oak decline (AOD), a bacterial infection working in association with a bark beetle, *Agrilus biguttatus* that can lead to the death of a mature tree within four to five years. Action Oak is an initiative, bringing together a range of professionals in the tree sector, growing and working with oak, including scientists, foresters, landowners, growers and many more raising vital funds for further research and monitoring to help protect our oak trees.

We must not lose this iconic tree from our landscape. It would be tragic and irresponsible of us all if we allowed the oak to succumb to these threats and would have a serious impact on our well-being, economy, environment and all the species that the oak supports and depends on. These trees are very photogenic at any time of the year in any season or weather and this book of exhibition quality photographs is a celebration of the oak and everything that it stands for. We must do all that is possible to prevent the further decline in the health of the oak in our treescape. The proceeds from the sale of this beautiful book will go towards further research that we need to increase our understanding in order to preserve them for future generations to enjoy.

ALAN PRICE

Oak Sunrise
Criccieth, Gwynedd, Wales

📷 Nikon D7100, Nikkor 18-55mm lens, 1/640sec at f/8, ISO 200. Monopod. Post-capture: converted to monochrome.

*It was a misty winter morning when the first light of the sun illuminated the landscape,
highlighting the bare and intricate form of this specimen oak tree.*

I spent a day photographing Epping Forest and was just about to leave when I noticed a beautiful blue and pink sky forming. I rushed back to one of my favourite locations just in time to capture this ancient oak tree reflected in the water and framed by the sky. There was a slight wintry chill in the air, which I think comes across in the scene.

MARION SIDEBOTTOM

2ND PLACE

Ancient Oak Reflection
Epping Forest, Greater London, England

📷 Sony α7R II, Sony 24-240mm lens, 1/50sec at f/7.1, ISO 500. Post-capture: basic image management.

JOHN GLOVER

Ancient Sessile Oak
Cowdray Park, Sussex, England

📷 Nikon D3X, Nikkor 28-70mm lens, 1/60sec at f/11, ISO 100. Tripod, cable release. Post-capture: basic image management.

An oak tree as ancient as this one has a kind of power and presence that is undeniable. More sculptural than any work of art, it needs to be touched, examined and experienced so that its history and our own relationship to nature can be more keenly felt.

CLARE PARK

Oak Trees in Winter
Surrey, England

📷 Nikon D800, Nikon 85mm lens, 1/200sec at f/13, ISO 200. Post-capture: basic image management.

These three beautiful oak trees, overlooking a quiet lane in Surrey, provided me with real solace during the three years I was caring for my parents. They represented the three of us. On my way home I used to drive to the location and sit quietly in my car and just be in their presence. I photographed them during the seasons but I never walked across the field. They remain to this day a place completely connected to my mother. They are unwavering in their strength and truly beautiful – just like her.

ANNA CURNOW

FINALIST

Misty Wistman's Wood
Wistman's Wood, Dartmoor National Park, England

📷 Canon EOS 5D Mark III, Canon 17-40mm lens, 0.8sec at f/16, ISO 200. Tripod. Post-capture: basic image management.

This ancient dwarf oak woodland is one of the most beautiful and most magical of oak tree environments.

MARIE DAVEY

FINALIST

Protective Canopy
Newlands Corner, Surrey, England

📷 Sony α7R II, Sony 24-70mm lens, 1/640sec at f/4, ISO 100. Post-capture: basic image management.

A couple stop to have a rest and admire the view, underneath the shelter of an old oak tree.

ANDREW LAWSON

Finalist

Devon Valley Oak
Devon, England

📷 Canon EOS 5D Mark II, Canon 45mm tilt-shift lens, 1/6sec at f/22, ISO 320. Tripod. Post-capture: basic image management.

Down in a secluded valley an ancient oak tree was growing beside a gently flowing stream.

ActionOak
PROTECTING OUR OAK TREES

DAVID CLARKE

FINALIST

Teenage Oak
Danbury Common, Essex,
England

📷 Fujifilm X-T10, Fujinon 18-
55mm lens, 1/12sec at f/16,
ISO 800. Tripod. Post-capture:
basic image management.

*This young oak should have
many, many years of growth
ahead of it. The morning
light imparts a sense of hope
for its future.*

MARION SIDEBOTTOM

FINALIST

On the Edge of Black-a-Tor Copse
Black-a-Tor Copse, Dartmoor, England

📷 Sony α7R II, Sony 16-35mm lens, 1/250sec at f/8, ISO 200.
Post-capture: basic image management.

After spending a few magical hours in Black-a-Tor Copse (an ancient high-altitude oak woodland) I started the walk along the West Okement River back to the car. A few remnants of the forest remain next to the river and I came across this beautiful wind-blown oak, which was just revealing its autumn colours.

ActionOak
PROTECTING OUR OAK TREES

MARION SIDEBOTTOM

Highly Commended

Great Windsor Oak
Windsor Great Park, Windsor, England

📷 Sony α7R II, Samsung 12mm lens, 1/25sec at f/8, ISO 100. Tripod. Post-capture: basic image management.

During a visit to the park I took this picture of an ancient oak tree holding court with its subjects. Windsor Great Park is a Royal Park of 4,500 acres and it is an important site for ancient and veteran oak trees in the UK.

GILLY HOPSON ▲

Winter Oaks
Whatcombe, Dorset, England

📷 Fujifilm X-T2, Fujinon 18-135mm lens, 1/40sec at f/6.4, ISO 400. Post-capture: basic image management.

A group of young oak trees were bravely weathering the ferocity of a severe snow storm.

CHRIS BESTALL

Millennium Oak IV
Monkland Common, Herefordshire, England

📷 Fujifilm X-T2, Fujinon 16-55mm lens, 1/100sec at f/10, ISO 200. Post-capture: basic image management.

This young oak was clinging to its last remaining leaves, midwinter on a Herefordshire common.

TIMOTHY SMITH

Square Oak
Hatfield Forest, Essex, England

📷 Canon EOS 6D, Canon 24-105mm lens, 1/25sec at f/11, ISO 100. Tripod. Post-capture: basic image management.

Situated in a Site of Special Scientific Interest, the bulk of this fine oak tree was perfectly suited to a square crop format.

DAVID CLARKE

Good Morning Oak
National Trust Hatfield Forest, Essex, England

📷 Fujifilm XT-1, Fujinon 55-200mm lens, 1/450sec at f/11, ISO 200. Tripod. Post-capture: basic image management.

Bathed in mist and glorious morning sunshine the promise of a new day is fulfilled.

NIGEL MCCALL

HIGHLY COMMENDED

Oak at Dryslwyn in Winter
Dryslwyn, Carmarthenshire, Wales

📷 Canon EOS 1DS Mark III, Canon 24-105mm lens, 0.8sec to 8sec at f/18, ISO 100. Tripod. Post-capture: merged three images together in Photomatix Pro, basic image management.

Viewed from the bridge at Dryslwyn this oak tree dominates the view up the River Towy. The photo was taken at dawn after many days of constant below-freezing temperatures when the Towy Valley was in the grip of an unusually deep frost.

BEN HIRST

Flooded Oaks
Wainlode, Gloucestershire, England

📷 Canon EOS 5DS, Canon 16-35mm lens, 1/40sec at f/11, ISO 640. Tripod. Post-capture: basic image management.

The magnificent spectrum of a new morning created the perfect backdrop for this group of oak trees on the banks of the River Severn.

ANDREW LAWSON

Ancient Oaks on a Misty Autumn Morning
Blenheim Palace, Oxfordshire, England

📷 Canon EOS 5D Mark II, Canon tilt-shift 45mm lens, 1/100sec at f/8, ISO 200. Tripod. Post-capture: basic image management.

I photographed these ancient oak trees on a misty autumn morning in the grounds of Blenheim Palace, the landscape of which was designed by Capability Brown and today is a UNESCO World Heritage Site.

SIMON LEA

Autumn Mist
Warley Woods, West Midlands, England

📷 Nikon D7000, Nikkor 18-55mm lens, 0.5sec at f/16, ISO 100. Tripod, remote release. Post-capture: basic image management.

A gentle mist was swirling around the base of these oak trees, the leaves of which were just beginning to change colour, signalling the start of autumn.

JULIETTE WILES ▲

COMMENDED

Oak Tree Silhouette II
Richmond Park, London, England

📷 Canon EOS 70D, Canon 17-85mm lens, 1/800sec at f/8, ISO 400.

A clear January morning offered the perfect opportunity to capture a fascinating silhouette of this oak tree in Richmond Park.

SIANA EVERTON

COMMENDED

Guardian of the Forest
Sherwood Forest, Nottinghamshire, England

📷 Nikon D3400, Nikkor 18-55mm lens, 1/800sec at f/4.2, ISO 400.

Capturing the essence of pareidolia, this image portrays an ancient guardian watching over the forest, staff in hand.

SIMON HADLEIGH-SPARKS

Commended

Acorns
Syon Park Gardens, London, England

📷 Canon EOS 5D Mark III, Canon 50mm lens, 1/10sec at f/16, ISO 100. Tripod. Post-capture: basic image management.

I wanted to celebrate the simple beauty of the acorn and the vast potential that lies within.

ALAN PRICE
Commended

Autumn Acorn
Criccieth, Gwynedd, Wales

📷 Nikon D7100, Nikkor 18-55mm lens, 1/60sec at f/11, ISO 100. Tripod. Post-capture: converted to monochrome.

This autumn acorn was seconds away from falling to the ground and beginning its spectacular journey of growth once again.

JOHN GLOVER

COMMENDED

Oak Tree at Charlwood Norman Church
Charlwood, Surrey, England

📷 Nikon D3X, Nikkor 24-70mm lens, 1/100sec at f/8, ISO 100. Tripod, cable release.
Post-capture: basic image management.

It was November when I took this photograph of an oak tree at the edge of a churchyard, right next to the village war memorial. People had chosen to place their Remembrance Day crosses at the base of this tree rather than the official memorial, perhaps because of an instinctual and powerful emotional connection with the oak tree.

DAVID CLARKE

COMMENDED

King Oak
Danbury Lakes, Essex, England

📷 Fujifilm XT-1, Fujinon 18-55mm lens, 1/10sec at f/8, ISO 200. Tripod. Post-capture: basic image management.

This huge oak acts as a guardian alongside this woodland path at Danbury Lakes. I chose a black and white capture to emphasise the detail and shape of its massive limbs.

SIMON LEA

COMMENDED

Burning Oak
Warley Woods, West Midlands, England

📷 Nikon D750, Nikkor 25-85mm lens, 0.8sec at f/14, ISO 100. Tripod, remote release, neutral density graduated filter. Post-capture: basic image management.

A blazing sunset made for a dramatic image of this landmark oak tree.

SUSAN LANG

COMMENDED

Evening Walk
Cheltenham, England

📷 Fujifilm X-T2, 16-55mm lens, 1/30sec at f/9, ISO 1000. Tripod, remote release app.
Post-capture: basic image management.

This is one of two old oak trees in a field on the edge of Cheltenham that is popular with local people. On warm summer evenings teenagers gather under the trees, while on rainy days the trees provide shelter for dog walkers. As well as its importance to the community, to me this tree represents the fight for survival. Someone set fire to the inside of the tree in the past; thankfully it survived, but the fire left a large blackened hole in the trunk.

SIMON LEA

COMMENDED

Sunburst Oak
Warley Woods, West Midlands, England

📷 Nikon D7000, Nikkor 18-55mm lens, 1/20sec at f/18, ISO 100. Tripod, remote release. Post-capture: basic image management.

The dazzling early morning autumn sun was rising behind this oak tree, creating a spectacular sunburst.

CAROLYNE BARBER

COMMENDED

Oak Trees in Waiting
Epping Forest, Greater London, England

📷 Nikon D7000, Helios 50mm lens, 1/125sec at f/2, ISO 400. Post-capture: basic image management.

On my morning walk through Epping Forest I could see the forest floor was scattered with beautiful acorns. Acorns are such beautiful seeds, full of fairy tales and nostalgia, a reminder of my childhood days when acorns were collected as little pieces of treasure.

ActionOak
PROTECTING OUR OAK TREES

DAVID CLARKE

COMMENDED

Morning Oak
National Trust Hatfield Forest, Essex, England

📷 Fujifilm XT-1, 18-55mm lens, 0.7sec at f/11, ISO 200. Tripod. Post-capture: added vignette, basic image management.

The mist and clear morning sky made for a perfect background as well as signalling an auspicious start to the day.

DEBBIE GREEN

COMMENDED

Through Snowfall
Greater London, England

📷 Olympus OM-2 (35mm film camera), Tamron 60-300mm lens, 1/15sec at f/8, ISO 400.

The falling snow emphasised a feeling of passing time. I contemplated how many more winters this oak tree would continue to see, long after we've passed.

Patrons of Renown

The oak tree has touched the lives of people everywhere across the UK. This section features photographs from patrons of renown, who like all of us, have a deep affinity with the oak tree. Action Oak would like to thank all patrons for sharing their images and supporting the initiative.

STEVEN CHESHIRE

Favourite image of Jon Snow, Chairman of the Heart of England Forest

ALAN TITCHMARSH

Broadcaster, Plantsman

SIR WILLIAM WORSLEY

Chair of the National Forest Company,
Government's Tree Champion

TONY KIRKHAM

Head of Arboretum and Horticultural Services, Royal Botanic Gardens, Kew

MICHAEL AGEL

Celebrity Photographer

MICHAEL AGEL

Celebrity Photographer

ADRIAN HOUSTON

Photographer

ADRIAN HOUSTON

Photographer

ADRIAN HOUSTON

Photographer

CHARLES SAINSBURY-PLAICE

Photographer

CHARLES SAINSBURY-PLAICE

Photographer

JOANNA LUMLEY

Actress

EDWARD PARKER

Trust Manager, Springhead Trust

EDWARD PARKER

Trust Manager, Springhead Trust

EDWARD PARKER

Trust Manager, Springhead Trust